TIMELINE SCIENCE:
THE ICE AGE

Silver Dolphin

Silver Dolphin Books

An imprint of Printers Row Publishing Group
A division of Readerink Distribution Services, LLC
10350 Barnes Canyon Road, Suite 100, San Diego, CA 92121
www.silverdolphinbooks.com

Copyright © 2017 Silver Dolphin Books

All rights reserved. No part of this publication may be reproduced, distributed, or transmitted in any form or by any means, including photocopying, recording, or other electronic or mechanical methods, without the prior written permission of the publisher, except in the case of brief quotations embodied in critical reviews and certain other noncommercial uses permitted by copyright law.

Printers Row Publishing Group is a division of Readerlink Distribution Services, LLC.
Silver Dolphin Books is a registered trademark of Readerlink Distribution Services, LLC.

All notation of errors or omissions should be addressed to Silver Dolphin Books, Editorial Department, at the above address.

ISBN: 978-1-62686-946-2

Manufactured, printed, and assembled in China.
21 20 19 18 17 1 2 3 4 5

Written by Emily Rose Oachs
Designed by Dynamo Limited

Image Credits:
Images copyright Thinkstock, Superstock, Inc., Claude Valette, Monnier, HTO, Flickr API, Sergiodlarosa, Riku64, Jaap Rouwenhorst, WolfmanSF, Momotarou2012, FunkMonk, Nobu Tamura, Creator:Dmitry Bogdanov, Kevmin, DFoidl, Drow male, Steven G. Johnson, Chphe, Arent, Bering Land Bridge National Preserve, Rainer Lippert, Ghedoghedo, John Gurche, Tim Evanson, Westfälisches Museum für Archäologie, Herne, Mauricio Antón, Ittiz, Franco Atirador, 3scandal0, Jack Versloot, Prof saxx, Dantheman9758, Ghedoghedo, Smokeybjb, Education Specialist, Xavier Vázquez, Claire Houck, Hermann Schaaffhausen, R. B. Forbes, doryfour, Eden, Janine and Jim, lora_313, Wallace63, Kevin Burkett, Stacy, Davide Meloni, Ra'ike, Karora, ArthurWeasley, Larry D. Moore, Paul Hudson, Cyclonaut, Images of marsupial lion, megalania, palorchestes, dire wolf, short-faced bear, incredible teratorn, giant beaver, toxodon, megatherium americanum, macrauchenia patachonica, hippidion, yesterday's camel, Harlan's ground sloth, American cheetah, cave hyena, giant moa, diprotodon, megaloceros, straight-tusked elephant, saber-toothed cat, steppe lion, narrow-nosed rhinoceros, steppe bison © Roman Uchytel.

Image of frozen steppe lion cubs © The Siberian Times.

Every effort has been made to contact copyright holders for the images in this book. If you are the copyright holder of any uncredited image herein, please contact us at Silver Dolphin Books, 10350 Barnes Canyon Road, Suite 100, San Diego, CA 92121.

CONTENTS

WHAT IS AN ICE AGE?

An **ice age** is a long period where Earth has continental ice sheets at the north and south poles for millions of years. We are currently in an ice age. Ice ages aren't always cold and icy. They also have periods of warmer weather that melt the ice sheets. These thaws are called **interglacial periods**. The temperatures may warm, but **glaciers** never fully melt.

Earth has experienced five major ice ages. The most recent is called the Quaternary Ice Age, and it began 2.58 million years ago and continues today.

Glaciers are massive sheets of ice that cover land. The largest are called ice sheets, and they can cover entire continents.

Glaciers start out as a layer of snow. Cold temperatures keep the snow from melting. Fresh snow falls and crushes the bottom layer of snow. The weight of the new snow turns the bottom layer into ice. As more fresh snow falls, more of the older snow turns into ice. This thick layer of ice becomes a glacier.

The Pleistocene Epoch

About 2.58 million years ago, Earth was changing. The planet was cooling after a few million years of relatively warm temperatures. Ice sheets already covered Antarctica and areas in the Arctic, but they began to spread across other parts of the world. This marked the start of the Quaternary Ice Age and the Pleistocene Epoch. The Pleistocene lasted for more than 2 million years.

North Pole

South Pole

MAJOR ICE AGES TIMELINE

Huronian Ice Age   2.4 billion years ago to 2.1 billion years ago

The Huronian Ice Age is the earliest known ice age. At the time, life on Earth was limited to single-celled organisms. Extremely cold temperatures reigned across the planet. At times, much of Earth was shrouded in ice.

Cryogenian Ice Age   850 million years ago to 630 million years ago

No other ice age experienced the same levels of deep freeze as the Cryogenian Ice Age. Even its name, Cryogenian, means "birth of cold." Geologists believe that glaciers reached the equator, and evidence suggests that ice sheets may have covered most of the planet. As a result, Earth during this period earned the nickname "Snowball Earth."

Andean-Saharan Ice Age   460 million years ago to 420 million years ago

During the Andean-Saharan Ice Age, South America, Africa, and other southern continents were joined in one supercontinent now known as Gondwana. The glaciers of this ice age stretched across South America and today's Sahara Desert in Africa. Although less severe, this ice age brought about the second-largest mass animal extinction in history, with more than four-fifths of Earth's species dying out.

Gondwana

Karoo Ice Age   360 million years ago to 260 million years ago

During the Karoo Ice Age, large ice sheets built up on Gondwana in the southern hemisphere. Today, much evidence of this glaciation exists in South Africa. The Ice Age is named for a region in the southern part of South Africa.

Quaternary Ice Age   2.58 million years ago to present

The Quaternary Ice Age is today's ice age. Other ice ages stretched for tens of millions of years or more, but the Quaternary Ice Age has lasted less than 3 million years. Global warming caused by humans is affecting cycles of this Ice Age and may bring the period to an early, unnatural end.

					CRYOGENIAN	KAROO	
					850—630 million years ago	360—260 million years ago	
2.5	2	1.5	1	0.5			present
HURONIAN					ANDEAN SAHARAN	QUATERNARY	
2.4—2.1 billion years ago					460—420 million years ago	2.58 million years ago—present	

5

WHY DO ICE AGES OCCUR?

Scientists believe a combination of factors brings about ice ages. One key contributor is the location of the continents. The position of the continents has not always been where they are today. **Plate tectonics** cause the continents to shift positions over long periods. Three hundred million years ago, that movement drew all the continents together to form a single supercontinent now called Pangaea. At other times, plate tectonics have separated the continents from each other.

These rearrangements can influence the start of ice ages as land moves closer to the poles. The poles are cold because they don't get any direct sunlight. Land near the poles makes ice more likely to form and remain. The difference between temperatures at the poles and the equator increases. These temperature extremes between the poles and the equator are necessary for an ice age to occur.

Shifting continents also alter the way water flows in the ocean. They open up new passageways that change the route of ocean currents. Ocean currents move warm water around the planet, bringing it to cooler areas. Changing ocean currents alter which parts of the world receive warm water, changing how heat is distributed on Earth.

Pangaea

North American Plate

Juan de Fuca Plate

Eurasian Plate

Arabian Plate

Indian Plate

Philippine Sea Plate

Pacific Plate

Pacific Plate

Caribbean Plate

Cocos Plate

African Plate

Nazca Plate

South American Plate

Australian Plate

Scotia Plate

Antarctic Plate

Within ice ages, the planet cycles through periods of longer, cooler glacial periods and shorter, warmer interglacial periods. Three main factors combine to affect this.

Orbit

One factor is the shape of Earth's orbit around the Sun. Earth's orbit does not follow a perfect circle around the Sun. Instead, Earth has an oval-shaped orbit, but sometimes it may be more oval-shaped, and other times, it may be more circular. A more oval-shaped orbit draws Earth farther away from the Sun. When this happens, snow and ice are less likely to melt during the summer. This can help lead to the formation of glaciers. Earth's orbit goes from oval-shaped to more circular and back about every 100,000 years.

Tilt

Another factor is the angle of Earth's tilt. Earth is naturally tilted, but that tilt can increase or decrease. If the angle of Earth's tilt decreases, then summer temperatures drop near the poles. This allows less snow and ice to melt during the summer. The increase and decrease of the tilt happens in cycles of about 41,000 years.

Precession

The third factor is Earth's wobble as it spins, or precession. Over about 26,000 years, Earth wobbles between pointing in one direction, toward the North Star, and pointing in a different direction, toward the star Vega. As a result, Earth reaches the closest point to the Sun at different times each year. Sometimes Earth is closest to the Sun in summer, and other times it is closest in winter. These shifts affect how much warmth Earth receives from the Sun at different times of the year.

FEEDBACK

Glaciers and ice sheets also decrease the amount of warmth Earth receives from the Sun. The ground is better able to absorb the Sun's energy, while sunlight bounces off snow and ice. As glaciers and ice sheets grow, more of the Sun's warmth is reflected into space. This creates even more cooling on the planet.

EARTH IN THE QUATERNARY ICE AGE: 2.58 MILLION YEARS AGO

During glacial periods, ice covered almost one-third of Earth's land. Ice sheets could grow more than two miles thick. No continent was left without ice. In the southern hemisphere, glaciers formed on the mountain peaks of Africa, Australia, and South America. All of Antarctica was covered by an ice sheet.

Cold periods struck the north the hardest. Large portions of North America and Eurasia were locked under ice sheets. There, the frozen landscape could stretch more than 100 miles south of the glacier's edge. Ice sheets act like water—they move across land by oozing and flowing. As they move, they scrape the land below them, reforming it.

At the height of the Ice Age, average temperatures were about 9°F lower than they are today. The edges of the ice sheets were even colder. There, average temperatures could have dropped to 36°F cooler than today.

ANIMALS AND HABITATS

The planet's climate completely changed during the Quaternary Ice Age. Quite a bit of Earth's water was frozen in the ice sheets. Cold, frozen deserts with few trees, called tundra, formed near the ice sheets.

Saiga antelope

Earth at this time would have been hard to recognize. Lakes stood in regions that are now hot and dry. In some places, today's forests were once tundra. Prehistoric swamps are now deserts. Some areas that are now wide prairies were once underwater. Regions that are underwater today were at times sprawling **steppes**.

Earth in the Quaternary Ice Age was not just a frozen world. Vast populations of animals lived south of the ice sheets. There, the landscape was not just ice. Steppes, grasslands, forests, and swamps gave homes to some of the most unique beasts to walk the planet.

Woolly mammoth

QUATERNARY ICE AGE TIMELINE

EARLY PLEISTOCENE
2.58 million—781,000 years ago

LATE PLEISTOCENE
126,000—11,700 years ago

| 2.5 | 2 | 1.5 | 1 | 0.5 | present |

millions of years ago

MIDDLE PLEISTOCENE
781,000—126,000 years ago

HOLOCENE
11,700 years ago
—present

EARLY PLEISTOCENE: GIANTS OF THE ICE AGE

The defining animals of the Quaternary Ice Age were its megafauna. These jumbo-sized animals roamed all over Earth. Mammoths, mastodons, woolly rhinoceroses, and saber-toothed cats are some of the most famous megafauna.

A large size helped these animals survive. For some, their size helped them stay warm. It protected them against the Quaternary Ice Age's bitter cold. Others needed their size to defend against predators. As those animals grew larger, their predators sometimes increased in size, too.

Arctodus simus "Short-Faced Bear"

Dates: 1.8 million—11,700 years ago
Range: North America
Habitat: Grasslands, steppe tundra, forests
Height: 5 feet (at shoulder)
Weight: 1,760 pounds
Diet: Bison, muskoxen, caribou, ground sloths

The short-faced bear was a common sight across the United States and Canada toward the end of the Pleistocene. It was the largest carnivore on land at the time, and it is also considered the largest bear to ever live. Short-faced bears had legs longer than those of most other bears. This means they may have been fast runners, helping them quickly chase after prey. However, some scientists believe that the bear may also have been a scavenger. It would have eaten the remains of animals that other predators killed. Either way, the jaws and teeth of the short-faced bear show that it was well-adapted to eat meat.

Short-Faced Bear

Glyptodont

Glyptodontinae: Glyptodonts

Dates: 3 million—11,700 years ago
Range: North America, South America
Habitat: Open forests and grasslands
Height: 10 feet
Weight: 2,000 pounds
Diet: Grasses

Glyptodonts were relatives of the modern armadillo. About 1,800 bony plates formed around the bodies of the glyptodonts. Even their tails were covered in armored plates. Some species had clubs at the end of their tails, which they could use to strike other animals. These features gave the massive, slow-moving animal protection from predators. However, saber-toothed cats occasionally attacked glyptodonts.

Ailornis incredibilis "Incredible Teratorn"

Dates: about 3 million—20,000 years ago
Range: North America
Habitat: Open grasslands
Wingspan: Up to 18 feet
Weight: 50 pounds
Diet: Carrion (dead animals), small animals

The incredible teratorn is part of a family of massive prehistoric birds and is related to condors. It had a wide wingspan and was among the largest birds to fly. The bird hunted small animals like rabbits and squirrels, but it would also scavenge on dead and dying animals of all sizes.

Incredible Teratorn

Castoroides ohioensis Giant Beaver

Dates: 3 million—11,700 years ago
Range: North America
Length: 7 feet
Weight: Up to 275 pounds
Habitat: Woodlands, swamps
Diet: Leaves, cattails

Giant Beaver

The giant beaver had large back feet but short hind legs. These traits made the giant beaver move awkwardly on land. However, the animal was an excellent swimmer and spent most of its life in water. It likely had a paddle-shaped tail like modern beavers, but this tail was longer and narrower. Its teeth were ridged with blunt and rounded tips. It is possible that the giant beaver neither chewed through trees nor built dams as modern beavers do.

EARLY PLEISTOCENE 2.58 million—781,000 years ago				LATE PLEISTOCENE 126,000—11,700 years ago	
2.5	2	1.5	1	0.5	present

millions of years ago

MIDDLE PLEISTOCENE
781,000—126,000 years ago

HOLOCENE
11,700 years ago —present

Glyptodonts & Giant Beavers

Incredible Teratorn

Short-Faced Bear

11

INTERGLACIAL MIGRATIONS

Not all Ice Age animals were accustomed to living in the cold. Many animals of the Pleistocene lived far south of the glaciers. There, warmer forests, grasslands, and swamps filled the landscape. Animals adapted to warmer weather made their homes in these milder climates.

The world froze and thawed as many as 30 times during the Quarternary Ice Age. With each thaw, the climate changed drastically. Warmer temperatures melted the glaciers. In some areas, frozen steppes became lush forests. Swamps and wetlands appeared farther north than before. More moisture and warmer temperatures allowed these habitats to form.

The changes brought massive animal migrations. Animals adapted to warmer weather could spread north as the glaciers moved away. Their habitats expanded, allowing them room to roam. Monkeys made their way into Europe. Camels and ground sloths lived in the Arctic.

Macaca sylvanus "Barbary Macaque"

Dates: 5.5 million years ago—present
Range: Europe, Africa
Habitat: Forest
Length: 28 inches
Weight: Up to 26 pounds
Diet: Bark, fruit, leaves, roots

The Barbary macaque is a tailless monkey. It remains the only macaque to ever live in Europe. During glacial periods of the Quaternary Ice Age, it lived in southern portions of the continent, such as in Italy and Spain. Some even made it into what would become modern-day England. Barbary macaques are social animals, usually living in groups of about 30 to 40 males and females. In the colony, males help to care for the young. Pouches inside a Barbary macaque's cheeks offer storage while searching for food. Their cheeks can store as much bark, fruit, leaves, and other vegetation as their stomach can hold.

EARLY PLEISTOCENE 2.58 million—781,000 years ago					LATE PLEISTOCENE 126,000—11,700 years ago
2.5	2	1.5	1	0.5	present

millions of years ago

MIDDLE PLEISTOCENE
781,000—126,000 years ago

HOLOCENE
11,700 years ago —present

Barbary Macaque

GLACIAL MIGRATIONS

Permafrost is ground that remains permanently frozen. It occurs in areas that have long periods of icy cold temperatures. Permafrost can extend deep below the surface. In warmer months, the upper parts may thaw. Yet farther underground, the ground remains frozen. In North America, permafrost in the Quaternary Ice Age could stretch for more than 100 miles south of the ice sheets. In Europe, the permafrost continued even farther south.

Some animals were built to survive on the permafrost. They had features, such as thick coats and large bodies, that kept them warm. Melting glaciers left behind milder, more temperate climates. These animals were not made to live in warmer weather, so they sometimes migrated north to live near permafrost.

Urocitellus parryii "Arctic Ground Squirrel"

Dates: 2.5 million years ago—present
Range: Asia, Europe, North America
Habitat: Tundra, meadows, near water
Length: 13.5 inches
Weight: Less than 2 pounds
Diet: Flowers, seeds, leaves, roots, fruits

Groups of up to 50 Arctic ground squirrels live together underground. Long tunnels connect their burrows. They need at least three feet of thawed permafrost to dig their dens. Each fall, Arctic ground squirrels collect and store food, such as seeds. Then, they hibernate in their dens for up to eight months. During that time, they are able to drop their body temperature to below freezing. This helps them survive harsh winters. When they wake up, they eat their stored food. Outside their dens, Arctic ground squirrels call out warnings to other ground squirrels nearby. They earned their Inuit name, "sik-sik," from the warning sound they make. Ermine, grizzly bears, and hawks all prey on the Arctic ground squirrel.

Homotherium serum "American Scimitar Cat"

Dates: 1.5 million—28,000 years ago
Range: North America
Habitat: Tundra, steppe
Weight: Up to 510 pounds
Diet: Small and large animals

Scimitar cats had two long, sharp, front teeth. The species earned its name from the resemblance its teeth bear to the curved blade of a sword called a scimitar. The powerful jaws and strong, stocky bodies of scimitar cats made them tough predators. Long front legs let them briefly sprint after their prey. These traits helped them hunt and capture large animals. Families of scimitar cats likely lived together, making their homes in caves. Scientists discovered one Texas cave with fossils of scimitar cats and their young, along with fossils from hundreds of young mammoths. As a result, scientists believe that scimitar cats targeted young herbivores.

Vulpes lagopus "Arctic Fox"

Dates: 1.8 million years ago—present
Range: Asia, Europe, North America
Habitat: Tundra
Height: 11 inches (at shoulder)
Weight: Up to 20 pounds
Diet: Lemmings, sea birds, fish

A dense, white coat covers the bodies of Arctic foxes. This keeps the small mammal warm in temperatures as cold as –58°F. Its color also helps the Arctic fox hide from predators against the snow. In the summer, its coat changes to brown or gray to better blend in with the bare ground. Lemmings are the key prey for this species. But Arctic foxes also hunt grouse, geese, and, if they live near the coast, fish. Arctic foxes may also scavenge on the bodies of animals already dead, such as seals.

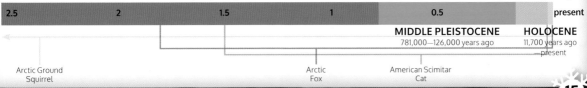

EARLY PLEISTOCENE					LATE PLEISTOCENE	
2.58 million—781,000 years ago					126,000—11,700 years ago	
2.5	2	1.5	1	0.5		present
				MIDDLE PLEISTOCENE	HOLOCENE	
				781,000—126,000 years ago	11,700 years ago—present	
Arctic Ground Squirrel		Arctic Fox		American Scimitar Cat		

AUSTRALIA'S MEGAFAUNA

The ice sheets of the Quaternary Ice Age mostly formed on the northern continents, but the Ice Age still affected Australia and its neighboring islands. Mountaintops in New Zealand held glaciers, while an ice sheet formed over the nearby island of Tasmania. Australia's climate shifted often between the glacial and interglacial periods. In glacial periods, the continent became dry, windy, and cool. Droughts made parts of the continent difficult for large animals to live in. The interglacial thaws brought warmer, more humid weather.

In Australia, animals depended on their large size to survive. But they did not have to rely on their size to keep warm. Instead, their size changed because of their diets. Plants had become less nutritious because of the changing climate. For plant-eaters, or herbivores, a larger size meant a slower metabolism. This, then, allowed them to eat, digest, and survive on tougher plants. Then predators, or carnivores, became larger to keep up with their prey, the herbivores.

Today, many of Australia's animals are unlike any others in the world. There, marsupials—like kangaroos and koalas—are among the most common mammals. The Ice Age was no different. Marsupials roamed the land, and Australia was home to some of the most unique animals on Earth.

Diprotodon optatum "Giant Wombat"

Dates: 1.6 million—46,000 years ago
Habitat: Plains, savannas, woodlands
Height: 5.5 feet (at shoulder)
Weight: Up to 6,100 pounds
Diet: Shrubs, nongrass flowering plants

Giant wombats were among the largest known marsupials to ever live. It is estimated that they ate 330 pounds of food each day! Sturdy legs allowed the giant wombat to carry around its bulky weight. Their teeth never stopped growing and helped the giant wombat tear up leaves, shrubs, and grasses. Like all marsupials, female giant wombats carried around their young in a pouch.

Thylacoleo carnifex "Marsupial Lion"

Dates: 2 million—46,000 years ago
Habitat: Open forests
Height: 2.4 feet
Weight: Up to 350 pounds
Diet: *Diprotodonts*, giant kangaroos, other medium to large animals

The marsupial lion was a stealthy predator. It would ambush unsuspecting prey, either by stalking from the ground or pouncing from a tree. Then it held the animal with its mouth. Using its powerful front legs and sharp, retractable thumb claws, the marsupial lion would then kill the animal.

Varanus priscus "Megalania"

Dates: 2.6 million—46,000 years ago
Habitat: Grasslands, open forests, woodlands
Length: 18 feet
Weight: Up to 1,300 pounds
Diet: Large mammals, snakes, birds

Megalania was a massive monitor lizard. It was the largest lizard known to have existed. It is related to today's Komodo dragon. Some scientists believe that, like the Komodo dragon, this giant lizard may have had venomous saliva. One bite from a *Megalania* could end in death. While hunting, *Megalania* used its sharp claws to attack diprotodons and other prey. A mouth full of serrated teeth also made it a fearsome predator. *Megalania* were rarer than Australia's other megafauna, but they were able to survive in a range of habitats.

Palorchestes azael "Palorchestes"

Dates: 5 million—46,000 years ago
Habitat: Marshes, eucalyptus woodlands
Diet: Bark, roots

The first scientist to find *Palorchestes* teeth believed he had discovered a large kangaroo. So he named the creature *Palorchestes*, which means "ancient leaper." *Palorchestes* was about the size of a cow and had strong front arms with sharp claws. Yet it did not use these to attack prey. Instead, *Palorchestes* was an herbivore, and it likely used its claws to dig or pull bark from trees. A long, flexible tongue, similar to that of a giraffe, helped it grasp and pull leaves from trees. *Palorchestes* likely inherited a backward-facing pouch from its wombat ancestors, who were digging animals. A backward-facing pouch would have prevented it from filling with dirt while digging.

EARLY PLEISTOCENE 2.58 million—781,000 years ago				LATE PLEISTOCENE 126,000—11,700 years ago	
2.5	2	1.5	1	0.5	present

millions of years ago

MIDDLE PLEISTOCENE 781,000—126,000 years ago

HOLOCENE 11,700 years ago—present

Megalania
Marsupial Lion

Palorchestes

Giant Wombat

17

MAMMOTHS AND MASTODONS

By one million years ago, the American mastodon and Columbian mammoth were North American neighbors. Herds of these animals shared the grasslands with each other and with other common Ice Age animals, such as dire wolves, bison, and saber-toothed cats.

Mastodon

Mammoth

MASTODON VS. MAMMOTH

Both the American mastodon and Columbian mammoth were related to modern-day elephants. At first glance, both could look similar with their trunks, large bodies, and long tusks. But key differences set them apart:

Mastodon

- Shorter and brawnier
- Flat head
- Shorter tusks
- Teeth featured two rows of round cones to break off branches and chew leaves, fruit, and twigs.

Mammoth

- Large, domed head
- Longer tusks
- Ridged teeth suited for grinding up grasses and tough plants

Mammut americanum "American Mastodon"

Dates: 3.75 million—11,700 years ago
Habitat: Woodlands, grasslands
Height: 10 feet (at shoulder)
Weight: Up to 12,000 pounds
Diet: Leaves, twigs, shrubs, bark

Shaggy fur covered the body of American mastodons, but the animals did not live near the ice sheets. It was too cold and dry for mastodons there. Instead, the animals made their homes in warmer, moister areas, as far north as modern-day Alaska and as far south as modern-day Honduras. Tusks appeared on both male and female mastodons. The males' tusks tended to be larger than those of females, reaching up to six feet in length.

Mammuthus columbi "Columbian Mammoth"

Dates: 1.1 million—11,700 years ago
Habitat: Grasslands
Height: 13 feet (at shoulder)
Weight: Up to 22,000 pounds
Diet: Grass, fruit

A layer of fur covered the bodies of Columbian mammoths. They lived in parts of North America with mild temperatures. Columbian mammoths were herbivores. It is estimated that they needed to eat about 770 pounds of grass each day to survive. To do this, they could have spent up to 18 hours grazing.

Their long tusks curved toward each other. They grew throughout the mammoth's life, and the tusks of males could reach 13 feet long. The mammoths may have used the tusks to sweep snow off the ground to get to the grass underneath and for defense from predators. Young mammoths faced threats from Ice Age carnivores, such as saber-toothed cats and American lions. In their herds, adults would protect the young from such threats.

EARLY PLEISTOCENE 2.58 million—781,000 years ago				LATE PLEISTOCENE 126,000—11,700 years ago	
2.5	2	1.5	1	0.5	present

millions of years ago

MIDDLE PLEISTOCENE 781,000—126,000 years ago

HOLOCENE 11,700 years ago —present

American Mastodon

Columbian Mammoth

SOUTH AMERICA IN THE MIDDLE PLEISTOCENE

Pleistocene South America was no stranger to ice. The Antarctic ice sheet expanded into southern South America. Ice caps formed across Patagonia. Glaciers grew along the Andes Mountains.

Near the ice, cold plains and grasslands crossed the landscape. Warmer grasslands and forests rose farther from the glaciers. At the continent's center stood the Amazon rain forest. This tropical rain forest dates back beyond the Pleistocene. In the Quaternary Ice Age, its territory grew during interglacial periods. Moisture in the air helped the rain forest grow.

A narrow strip of land called the Panamanian Isthmus, connected South America and North America. By the Pleistocene, the Americas had been connected for millions of years. The two continents shared some animals that migrated from one continent to another over the isthmus. The saber-toothed cat and tapir made the journey south. The capybara and armadillo traveled north. But Pleistocene South America was home to a diverse array of strange mammals. Many of them were unique to the continent.

Toxodon

Dates: 3.6 million—11,700 years ago
Range: South America
Habitat: Steppe, grasslands
Height: 5 feet (at shoulder)
Weight: Up to 2,420 pounds
Diet: Grass or leaves

Toxodons were common animals in Pleistocene South America. With sturdy, heavy bodies, they likely looked similar to the hippopotamuses and rhinoceroses of today. Curved upper teeth gave them the name Toxodon, which means "arched tooth." Gaps stood between these teeth and also separated the front teeth from the back molars. Toxodon's nostrils were placed high on its long nose, and it had wide, three-toed hoofs.

Megatherium americanum

Dates: about 781,000—8,000 years ago
Range: South America, North America
Habitat: Open woodlands
Weight: 8,800 pounds
Diet: Leaves, bark

Megatherium was one of the most massive ground sloths of the Ice Age. This gave the animal its name, which means "great beast." Large, formidable claws grew from its front paws. These allowed the animal to tear bark from trees or to strike back at predators. Megatherium most likely walked on all fours, but it could stand upright on its thick, muscular hind legs.

Macrauchenia patachonica

Dates: about 781,000—11,700 years ago
Range: South America
Habitat: Grasslands
Weight: Up to 2,400 pounds
Diet: Leaves, shrubs, grass

The name Macrauchenia means "long neck." Macrauchenia look similar to camels without a hump. The position of their nostrils suggests that they had a short trunk. Yet some scientists believe that instead of a trunk, Macrauchenia were able to seal their nostrils. Macrauchenia generally lived in dry areas prone to sandstorms. Sealing their nostrils would have kept them from breathing in dust. Macrauchenia were fast, agile runners. Their legs were specially adapted for quickly changing direction. The animals could easily dart away from saber-toothed cats and other predators.

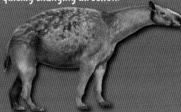

Hippidion

Dates: 2.5 million—11,700 years ago
Range: South America
Habitat: Open forests and grasslands
Weight: Up to 1,100 pounds
Diet: Grass, trees, shrubs

The first Hippidions appeared in Central or South America about 2.5 million years ago. Two different types of horses—Hippidion and *Equus*—lived in South America during the Quaternary Ice Age. Yet both died out around the end of the Pleistocene. Hippidions were different from *Equus* in that they had short, stocky bodies, and they were adapted to live more in open forests than in open areas. Like modern horse species, Hippidion was likely a fast runner.

	EARLY PLEISTOCENE 2.58 million—781,000 years ago					LATE PLEISTOCENE 126,000—11,700 years ago	
2.5	2	1.5	1		0.5		present
		millions of years ago			MIDDLE PLEISTOCENE 781,000—126,000 years ago		HOLOCENE 11,700 years ago —present
	Toxodon		Hippidion			*Macrauchenia*	*Megatherium*

NORTH AMERICA IN THE MIDDLE PLEISTOCENE

In the Middle Pleistocene, North America teemed with life. Its woodlands and grasslands were home to many large animals. The saber-toothed cat was one of the most feared. It was shorter than today's African lion, but almost twice its weight. The saber-toothed cat ruled the Quaternary Ice Age from 700,000 years ago until the end of the Pleistocene.

Two long, curved teeth gave the saber-toothed cat its name. A saber is a sword with a long, curved blade. A saber-toothed cat's teeth could grow to be seven inches long. Serrated edges helped the teeth cut through flesh.

Smilodon fatalis "Saber-toothed Cat"

Dates: 700,000—11,700 years ago
Range: North America, South America
Habitat: Woodlands, brushy plains, grasslands
Height: 3 feet (at shoulder)
Weight: Up to 750 pounds
Diet: Bison, deer, ground sloths, young mastodons and mammoths, and other large herbivores.

The saber-toothed cat's muscular body made it a powerful creature. This predator could take down some of the largest animals of the Quaternary Ice Age. Among its favorite meals were bison, deer, and young mammoths.

Saber-toothed cats were not built for running as some cats are, so they likely ambushed their prey. The cat would pin the animal down using its strong, thick arms. Or, its teeth could have delivered a killing blow. The cat would have opened its mouth wide and used its sharp teeth to bite into soft parts of its prey's body, such as the stomach or throat.

Scientists have discovered fossils from saber-toothed cats that show some became injured, but healed. This leads scientists to believe that saber-toothed cats lived together in groups. When one cat was injured, others would help care for it so it could survive.

Paramylodon harlani
"Harlan's Ground Sloth"

Dates: 1 million—11,700 years ago
Range: North America
Habitat: Grasslands near water
Height: 12 feet
Weight: Up to 3,500 pounds
Diet: Grass, herbs, roots

The Harlan's ground sloth moved awkwardly. It walked along the outside edge of its hind feet, while it put weight onto the knuckles. The body of a Harlan's ground sloth was built for defense. Tiny bones grew in the Harlan's ground sloth's skin, forming a kind of armor. Thick, strong front legs adorned with menacing claws gave it extra protection from predators.

Camelops hesternus
"Yesterday's Camel"

Dates: 600,000—11,700 years ago
Range: North America
Habitat: Grasslands, scrublands
Height: 7 feet (at shoulder)
Weight: Up to 1,750 pounds
Diet: Leaves, shrubs, flowers

Yesterday's camels looked similar to the camels of today. But yesterday's camels had longer legs and were much larger overall. Families of yesterday's camels likely joined together in small herds. They spread across western United States, reaching Alaska. The species ate grasses, and their long necks also allowed them to reach leaves high up in trees. Camels originated in North America millions of years ago. About 5 million years ago, or possibly earlier, they migrated across the Bering Land Bridge into Eurasia.

EARLY PLEISTOCENE 2.58 million—781,000 years ago			LATE PLEISTOCENE 126,000–11,700 years ago

2.5	2	1.5	1	0.5	present

millions of years ago

MIDDLE PLEISTOCENE
781,000—126,000 years ago

HOLOCENE
11,700 years ago
—present

Harlan's Ground Sloth

Saber—Toothed Cat

Yesterday's Camel

ICE AGE SERENGETI

Today, lions and cheetahs call Africa's Serengeti home. But Pleistocene North America was home to its own savanna animals. The American lion and American cheetah shared North America's grasslands in the middle Pleistocene.

These animals were some of North America's fiercest predators. Speed helped them chase down their favorite prey: pronghorns. American lions would stalk pronghorns before quickly attacking. Cheetahs took off sprinting after pronghorns to catch their next meal.

THE PRONGHORN'S PLEISTOCENE PREDATORS

Today, pronghorns are North America's fastest land animal. They can reach speeds of 60 miles per hour. Their Pleistocene predators were built for running, too. The threat from these predators helped the pronghorn's speed. Pronghorns spent thousands of years fleeing those predators. Over time, they gradually evolved to be faster and faster.

Today, no North American predators come close to reaching the pronghorn's speed. But today's pronghorns still race across the landscape as if Ice Age predators are right behind them.

Panthera atrox "American Lion"

Dates: 300,000—11,700 years ago
Habitat: Tundra, mountain forests, grasslands
Length: 8 feet
Weight: Up to 660 pounds
Diet: Bison, horses, camels, deer

American lions were greater in size—possibly 25 percent bigger—than today's African lions. Its long legs made it well-adapted for sprinting. It is estimated that American lions could run at speeds of up to 30 miles per hour. Because of their running ability, American lions most likely lived in open environments. These powerful hunters held their captured prey down with their strong front legs. Then, they targeted the throats of their prey, delivering a powerful bite with their muscular jaws. By the end of the Pleistocene, American lions had a wide range, stretching from North America to Peru.

Miracinonyx inexpectatus "American Cheetah"

Dates: 2.5 million—20,000 years ago
Habitat: Grasslands, open forests, mountains
Height: 33 inches (at shoulder)
Weight: 156 pounds
Diet: Pronghorns, mountain sheep, horses

Miracinonyx inexpectatus, the American cheetah's scientific name, means "wonderful unexpected" cheetah. With long, slender legs, the American cheetah's body was built to be a fast runner. Its nostrils were also large, allowing the animal to easily breathe while sprinting. Scientists believe that the American cheetah, with its amazing speed, was the animal that most helped pushed evolution to make the pronghorn become so fast.

Antilocapra americana "Pronghorn"

Dates: 1.8 million years ago—present
Habitat: Grasslands, open shrublands
Length: 5 feet
Weight: Up to 150 pounds
Diet: Grass, shrubs

Females are slightly smaller in size than males. Yet their curving, two-pronged horns are usually much shorter than males'. The horns of males may reach 12 inches or more in length, while those of females may only grow to 4 inches. Pronghorns prefer open areas. Their large eyes are positioned so they have a broad view of their surroundings. Not only can pronghorns sprint quickly at 60 miles per hour, but they are also long-distance runners. They can run for miles at a pace of about 30 miles per hour.

EARLY PLEISTOCENE 2.58 million—781,000 years ago				LATE PLEISTOCENE 126,000—11,700 years ago	
2.5	2	1.5	1	0.5	present

millions of years ago

MIDDLE PLEISTOCENE 781,000—126,000 years ago

HOLOCENE 11,700 years ago–present

American Cheetah — Pronghorn — American Lion

BUILT FOR THE COLD

Life just south of the ice sheets could be harsh. Temperatures were frigid, averaging 21°F. Yet there was little snow. Much of Earth's water was locked up in the ice sheets. So, areas near those ice sheets were very dry.

Woolly rhinoceros

Woolly mammoth

The woolly mammoth and woolly rhinoceros were two of the Quaternary Ice Age's most famous animals. They emerged about 300,000 years ago, during the middle Pleistocene. They lived on the freezing plains south of the ice sheets.

Both shared similar features to help cope with the cold. Woolly mammoths and woolly rhinoceroses had long, furry coats. Shorter, thicker fur made up their undercoats, which kept them extra warm. Small ears and short tails kept the animals from losing body heat. It is estimated that both animals also had to eat as much as 400 pounds of food a day!

Mammuthus primigenius "Woolly Mammoth"

Dates: about 300,000—11,700 years ago
Range: Asia, Europe, North America
Habitat: Tundra, steppe
Height: 10 feet (at shoulder)
Weight: 12,000 pounds
Diet: Grass

A woolly mammoth's outer layer of fur could grow to be 35 inches long! To keep warm, a layer of fat up to 3.5 inches thick helped insulate their bodies. A hump on their backs stored fat, which helped them survive in the cold. Long, curved tusks made woolly mammoths easy to identify. Mammoths may have used them to defend themselves against threats. Evidence also points to mammoths using them to clear ice from the ground to expose their food.

Herds of mammoths wandered the permafrost, grazing together. The young stayed near their mothers, relying on them for milk until about the age of three. Woolly mammoths likely first evolved in Siberia. From there, they spread out across Eurasia and over the Bering Land Bridge into North America.

Coelodonta antiquitatis "Woolly Rhinoceros"

Dates: about 350,000—11,700 years ago
Range: Asia, Europe
Habitat: Tundra, grasslands
Height: 5 feet (at shoulder)
Weight: Up to 2,500 pounds
Diet: Grass, lichen, moss

Two horns stood on the nose of a woolly rhinoceros. The front horn was long, flat, and on males, it could grow to be three feet long! Its flat shape helped the woolly rhinoceros sweep snow off the ground, so the animal could reach food. Males probably fought other male rhinos using their horns. Scientists believe they likely led solitary lives like modern African rhinos, living alone or in small groups.

| EARLY PLEISTOCENE | | | | LATE PLEISTOCENE | |
| 2.58 million—781,000 years ago | | | | 126,000—11,700 years ago | |

| 2.5 | 2 | 1.5 | 1 | 0.5 | present |

millions of years ago

MIDDLE PLEISTOCENE
781,000—126,000 years ago

HOLOCENE
11,700 years ago
—present

Woolly Rhinoceros

Woolly Mammoth

BERING LAND BRIDGE

During the Pleistocene, more of Earth's water was frozen than today, locked in far-reaching ice sheets. Less liquid water meant that Earth's sea level dropped considerably. At times, it reached 400 feet lower than it is today. Lower sea levels exposed land that had previously been underwater.

During interglacial periods, a narrow channel of water separated North America and Asia. But glacial periods brought lower sea levels that uncovered the Bering Land Bridge, a wide strip of land. It stretched about 1,000 miles north to south. The land bridge connected Alaska in North America to Siberia in Asia.

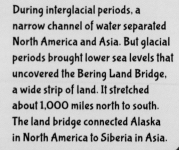

The Bering Land Bridge likely reached its widest about 20,000 years ago. But long before then, the Bering Land Bridge had become home to many animals. It was a flat, grassy area that was largely dry and untouched by ice, even at the height of the glacial periods. Mammoths, horses, and lions called the land bridge home.

For other animals, the land bridge was a route to a new continent. Camels, brown bears, mammoths, and many other animals crossed the land bridge.

Bison priscus "Steppe Bison"

Dates: 700,000—400 years ago
Date of Move: 160,000 years ago
Habitat: Grasslands, steppe
Weight: Up to 1,700 pounds
Diet: Grass, herbs

Steppe bison were about the same size as today's bison. Yet their curved horns were much larger. The horns on males could have stretched about 3 feet across, while females tended to have smaller horns. A hump also grew on their backs, underneath a black mane of hair. These bison lived in herds, feeding on grasses that covered the steppe. After migrating, they quickly spread across North America. Soon, they became the most common herbivorous megafauna in North America.

Ovibos moschatus "Tundra Muskox"

Dates: about 500,000 years ago—present
Date of Move: about 250,000 years ago
Habitat: Tundra
Height: 4 feet (at shoulder)
Weight: Up to 900 pounds
Diet: Grass, willow shoots, roots, moss, lichen

Muskoxen are well adapted to survive the cold. Their four-inch-thick shaggy coats keep them warm in temperatures well below freezing. The animal sheds its shorter, woollier undercoat as spring begins. The longer hair of the outer coat, called guard hair, remains throughout the year. Wide horns branch out from the foreheads of both males and females. Muskoxen are social animals, living in herds of up to 36. They work together to protect themselves from threats. When a predator approaches, the animals circle around their young and face outward. Predators, such as wolves and bears, are unable to break through the ring.

Rangifer tarandus "Caribou"

Dates: about 2 million years ago—present
Date of Move: 300,000 years ago
Habitat: Forests, tundra
Height: 5 feet (at shoulder)
Weight: Up to 700 pounds
Diet: Grass, mushrooms, lichen

Like muskoxen, caribou have a layered coat. The longer coat is made up of hollow guard hairs, while the undercoat is shorter and thicker. Caribou are known for their yearly migrations. Today's caribou may travel 600 miles to reach fresh feeding grounds. Unlike other types of deer, both the males and females grow antlers, although males' grow to be much larger. A caribou's wide hooves are useful tools, helping the animal walk across snowy or wet ground, or to paddle through water.

EARLY PLEISTOCENE 2.58 million—781,000 years ago				LATE PLEISTOCENE 126,000—11,700 years ago	
2.5	2	1.5	1	0.5	present

millions of years ago

MIDDLE PLEISTOCENE
781,000—126,000 years ago

HOLOCENE
11,700 years ago
present

Caribou

Steppe Bison

Tundra Muskox

A NEW ANIMAL: MODERN HUMANS

In the early Pleistocene, a new animal emerged in eastern Africa. Evidence suggests the earliest humans first roamed Africa's savannas about 2.4 million years ago. Other ancestors of humans, the early hominins, date back to as early as 7 million years ago.

The identifying characteristic of humans is their ability to walk upright on two legs. This ability, called bipedalism, is what sets humans apart from apes. Human ancestors developed this trait about 4 million years ago. Humans no longer needed to use their hands for movement. Therefore, walking upright would have allowed humans to use their hands to make and hold weapons and other tools.

As more time passed, early humans evolved into more complex animals. Along with using tools, humans' brains became larger. This gave them the ability to create language and culture. As a whole, humans developed skills and traits that would let them adapt to a variety of habitats and climates.

Modern humans, Homo sapiens, originated on Africa's savannas about 200,000 years ago. About 85,000 years ago, they moved into Asia. By 65,000 years ago, humans spread into Australia and, 45,000 years ago, they were in Europe. By the end of the Pleistocene, they had followed the Bering Land Bridge into the Americas.

The Fate of the Neanderthals

The Neanderthals did not survive the final glacial period. They died out about 40,000 years ago. At that time, modern humans and Neanderthals had shared Europe for about 5,000 years. Scientists believe that humans were better prepared to survive the Ice Age than the Neanderthals. They likely had technology and trade networks that helped them during particularly cold and difficult times. This allowed them to survive the Pleistocene while the Neanderthals could not. But scientists also note that humans and Neanderthals interbred. As a result, Neanderthals and humans merged into a single species. Decreased population and interbreeding led to the Neanderthals' disappearance.

Homo habilis

Dates: 2.4 million—1.4 million years ago
Range: Africa

The Homo habilis, meaning "handy man," was among the first of the Homo genus. Bones of this species were found surrounded by tools. Scientists believe the Homo habilis may have been the first in history to make stone tools. Based on the species' brain shape, scientists also think it is possible that the Homo habilis communicated using primitive language. The Homo habilis would have been smaller than modern humans, standing at up to 5 feet tall and weighing up to 100 pounds.

Homo erectus

Dates: 1.89 million—143,000 years ago
Range: Africa, Asia

Scientists believe that Homo erectus were the first humans to travel beyond Africa. They settled in two continents, moving as far east as China. The Homo erectus are linked to the first use of campfires. They likely gathered around the fire to cook food, where they probably socialized with others. The average Homo erectus stood up to 6 feet tall, and could weigh as much as 150 pounds. Protein from meat likely gave the large-brained Homo erectus enough energy to last through the day. Homo erectus are believed to have built the first cleavers and hand axes. Their sharp tools were able to tear through animal skins and were important advances in stone tool technology.

Homo neanderthalensis "Neanderthals"

Dates: 400,000—40,000 years ago
Range: Europe, Asia

Neanderthals often made their homes in caves, earning the nickname "cave men." They are the closest relative to modern humans. Their short, brawny bodies were built to survive the Ice Age in Europe. Wide noses let them breathe in and warm the cold, dry air. The average males were shorter than today's humans, at about 5.5 feet tall and 143 pounds. Yet fossils of Neanderthals' thick bones suggest that they were stronger than modern humans. A number of characteristics show the Neanderthals' sophistication, including their use of tools, shelter, and clothing. They are also believed to be the first humans to bury their dead. Neanderthals hunted some of the Pleistocene's megafauna. Reindeer, red deer, and woolly mammoths were all on the menu.

Homo sapiens "Modern Humans"

Dates: 200,000 years ago—present
Range: Africa, Asia, Australia, Europe, North America, South America

Modern humans are distinguishable by their taller, thinner frames and larger brains. They are social animals. Prehistoric humans are known for their creation of specialized tools, such as sewing needles, bows and arrows, and fishing hooks. Starting around 40,000 years ago, the culture of Homo sapiens started to become more sophisticated. In time, humans began to create artwork and build musical instruments. About 12,000 years ago, the first Homo sapiens shifted from being hunter-gatherers to farmers.

	EARLY PLEISTOCENE 2.58 million—781,000 years ago				LATE PLEISTOCENE 126,000—11,700 years ago
2.5	2	1.5	1	0.5	present
		millions of years ago		MIDDLE PLEISTOCENE 781,000—126,000 years ago	HOLOCENE 11,700 years ago—present
	Homo Habilis		Homo Erectus	Neanderthals	Modern Humans

HIPPOS IN BRITAIN

Europe in the glacial periods could be freezing cold. The British Isles were no different. During some glacial periods, ice sheets worked their way down, and parts of Britain became a frozen landscape. Yet interglacial Europe would grow to be very warm.

About 130,000 years ago, an interglacial period thawed the planet. In the British Isles, woodlands and savannas replaced the glaciers. From their homes in southern Europe, animals moved north and west to make their homes there. They crossed a land bridge that formed as sea levels dropped. It connected Britain to Europe's mainland during the Pleistocene.

Some unexpected animals made their way into the British Isles. Hippopotamuses today are best known for living beside African rivers. Yet these giants wallowed in the waters of interglacial Great Britain.

Hippopotamus amphibius "Hippopotamus"

Dates: 1.8 million years ago—present
Range: Europe, Africa (today)
Habitat: Rivers and coasts near grasslands
Height: Up to 5.4 feet
Weight: Up to 3,253 pounds
Diet: Grass

During glacial periods, Ice Age hippos lived in the Mediterranean. But interglacial periods drew them into Britain and Western Europe. Fossils have been found near the River Thames in the heart of London. Those Ice Age hippos survive today, although they only appear in Africa.

Large tusk-like teeth grow from the mouths of hippopotamuses. They grow much larger in males than females. They use these teeth to fight off threats. Herds of hippopotamuses rest in water during the day. Their bodies are built for this lifestyle. Their nostrils and eyes are located high on their heads. This allows them to breathe and see, even when the rest of their bodies are underwater.

Palaeoloxodon antiquus "Straight-Tusked Elephant"

Dates: 2.6 million—about 34,000 years ago
Range: Europe
Habitat: Woodlands
Height: 13 feet
Weight: 28,000 pounds
Diet: Leaves, branches, grass

During the last interglacial period, straight-tusked, (or forest), elephants were common sights in warmer areas of Europe. The last of the straight-tusked elephants left Britain about 120,000 years ago. They moved toward regions in southern Europe, such as Italy. Straight-tusked elephants were named for their tusks, which had only a slight curve.

Stephanorhinus hemitoechus "Narrow-Nosed Rhinoceros"

Dates: 2.6 million—126,000 years ago
Range: Asia, Europe
Habitat: Grasslands, some woodlands
Height: 7 feet tall
Weight: 6,600 pounds
Diet: Leaves, twigs

The narrow-nosed rhinoceros appeared as far east as Asia. Yet Europe was its common home. Caves along Britain's coast revealed remains from the animal, along with fossils from straight-tusked elephants.

EARLY PLEISTOCENE 2.58 million—781,000 years ago				LATE PLEISTOCENE 126,000—11,700 years ago	
2.5	2	1.5	1	0.5	present

millions of years ago

MIDDLE PLEISTOCENE 781,000—126,000 years ago

HOLOCENE 11,700 years ago present

Narrow-Nosed Rhinoceros

Straight-Tusked Elephant

Hippopotamus

THE LAST GLACIAL PERIOD: LATE PLEISTOCENE

For more than 2 million years, the planet alternated between periods of freeze and thaw. About 120,000 years ago, Earth was in the midst of another warm period, but it was nearing its end. Soon, the planet plunged into another glacial period. It was the last of the Pleistocene Epoch. It began about 110,000 years ago.

THE MAMMOTH STEPPE

The mammoth steppe was an important landscape of the last glacial period. It was a sprawling area of gently rolling land, covered by grasses and wildflowers. Few trees stood on the cool, dry landscape. The mammoth steppe stretched from Europe, through Asia, across the Bering Land Bridge, and into North America. A rich variety of animals—including mammoths, bison, and lions—called the mammoth steppe home.

For thousands of years, the planet became colder and colder. The peak of the last glaciation came 20,000 years ago. North American ice sheets stretched as far south as today's Wisconsin. Much of Europe was under ice.

Saiga tatarica "Saiga Antelope"

Dates: about 2 million years ago—present
Range: Asia, Europe, North America
Height: 30 inches
Weight: 75 pounds
Diet: Grass

The mammoth steppe was a cold and dusty place. But during the Ice Age, the large noses of saiga antelopes helped them breathe air, warming and filtering it. Today's saiga antelopes are only found on central Asia's steppes, but during the Pleistocene, they stretched across Eurasia and into northern North America. The open steppe allows saigas to spot predators and to sprint away, sometimes reaching speeds of 40 miles per hour. Only males have the distinctive horns. As many as 1,000 saiga antelope form herds. These herds migrate each winter to new feeding grounds.

Canis lupus "Gray Wolf"

Dates: 500,000 years ago—present
Range: Asia, Europe, North America
Length: 4.9 feet
Weight: 130 pounds
Diet: Bison, caribou, horses

Gray wolves were likely familiar predators on the mammoth steppe. In North America, two different populations of gray wolves existed. Near the Bering Land Bridge, gray wolves were adapted to have stronger bites. Scientists believe that these animals were both hunters and scavengers, and that they even ate bone. Those gray wolves went extinct at the end of the Pleistocene. Today's gray wolves are descendants of the gray wolves that lived in the continental United States. These highly social animals form packs of about ten or fewer.

| EARLY PLEISTOCENE 2.58 million—781,000 years ago | | | | LATE PLEISTOCENE 126,000—11,700 years ago |

| 2.5 | 2 | 1.5 | 1 | 0.5 | present |

millions of years ago

MIDDLE PLEISTOCENE 781,000—126,000 years ago

HOLOCENE 11,700 years ago—present

Saiga Antelope

Gray Wolf

LIFE IN CAVES

Many animals sought out caves to escape the Quaternary Ice Age's bitter cold. Outside, the world could be icy and frigid. But deep inside the caves, temperatures were less severe. They gave animals important protection.

Caves not only protected animals when they were living—they also protected them long after their deaths. Scientists have discovered troves of Ice Age animal remains in caves because caves' cool and moist conditions preserve the animals' remains!

Chauvet Cave

Discovered in France in 1994, Chauvet Cave was found by three explorers who stumbled upon the cave's passage, covered by rocks. Inside the cave the fossilized remains of cave bears were discovered. The cave bears would have hibernated in the cave. The skull of an ibex and the remains of two wolves were also uncovered. The walls and floor of the cave had scratches and footprints from the bears.

Natural Trap Cave

Located in Wyoming, the Natural Trap Cave is one of the richest sites in North America for Ice Age fossils. The cave is 80 feet deep and is more of a sinkhole. It became a deadly trap for animals because they would fall into the cave, unable to escape. Today, fossils of short-faced bears, bison, American lions, and mammoths have been found at the bottom.

CAVE INHABITANTS

Panthera leo spelaea "Steppe Lion"

Dates: 300,000—11,700 years ago
Range: Asia, Europe, North America
Habitat: Forests, grasslands
Height: 4.5 feet (at shoulder)
Diet: Deer, horses, reindeer, bison

Steppe lions are sometimes called "cave lions" because so many of their remains have been found in caves. Yet these predators likely did not live in caves. Instead, they most often lived and hunted in forests or on the steppe. They reached as far as North America and were possibly the ancestor to American lions.

Crocuta crocuta spelaea "Cave Hyena"

Dates: 300,000—11,700 years ago
Range: Asia, Europe
Habitat: Plains
Weight: 285 pounds
Diet: Horses, reindeer, ibex, scavenged cave bears

Cave hyenas took shelter in caves, using them as their dens. There, they may have raised their young and stored carcasses of animals they had killed. Evidence shows that cave hyenas and Neanderthals lived in the same caves, although at different times.

EARLY PLEISTOCENE 2.58 million—781,000 years ago				LATE PLEISTOCENE 126,000—11,700 years ago	
2.5	2	1.5	1	0.5	present
		millions of years ago		MIDDLE PLEISTOCENE 781,000—126,000 years ago	HOLOCENE 11,700 years ago —present

Steppe Lion & Cave Hyena

KINGDOMS OF THE DIRE WOLF

In the late Pleistocene, dire wolves hunted between present-day Bolivia to Canada. These predators were highly adaptable. They could live in a wide range of environments, from South America's savannas to the forests of North America. They likely traveled across these regions in packs similar to those of modern gray wolves.

Dire wolves were feared hunters, but their shorter legs likely prevented them from being as speedy as gray wolves. Still, their sturdy, muscular bodies helped them attack horses and young mastodons and mammoths. As a pack, dire wolves could take down even larger prey, such as an adult bison. Large teeth and strong jaws let dire wolves crush the bones of their prey.

Although dire wolves probably looked similar to gray wolves, their bodies would have been about 25 percent bigger. Dire wolves also had wider skulls but smaller brains than gray wolves.

Canis dirus "Dire Wolf"

Dates: 130,000—11,700 years ago
Range: North America, South America
Habitat: Wetlands, grasslands, forests
Height: 2.6 feet (at shoulder)
Weight: Up to 150 pounds
Diet: Bison, horses, ground sloths, mastodons, camels, and other large herbivores

Forested Tundra

In the late Pleistocene, dire wolves wandered the forested tundra south of the ice sheets. These cold, tundra areas of trees and shrubs occurred near North America's Great Lakes. Although the area was still dry, there was more moisture there than in the steppe tundra.

Habitat neighbors: Caribou, stag–moose, mammoths, scimitar cats

Spruce Parkland and Forest

The dire wolf's spruce parkland appeared farther south of the ice sheets, making it more temperate than the tundra. Spruce, pine, fir, and balsam would have towered overhead beside nearby open areas. Oaks became more common as the glaciers began to retreat. In this region, both animals that could withstand the bitter cold and animals adapted to warmer weather lived together.

Habitat neighbors: American mastodons, flat-headed peccaries, short-faced bear, giant beavers

Grasslands and Savannas

Grasslands appeared in North America, while drier savannas spread over parts of Central and South America. Few, if any, scattered trees stood on these open, dry regions, but diverse Ice Age wildlife called these areas home.

Habitat neighbors: Saber-toothed cats, ancient bisons, pronghorns, camels, glyptodonts

	EARLY PLEISTOCENE 2.58 million—781,000 years ago				LATE PLEISTOCENE 126,000—11,700 years ago	
2.5	2	1.5	1	0.5		present
		millions of years ago		MIDDLE PLEISTOCENE 781,000—126,000 years ago	HOLOCENE 11,700 years ago —present	

Dire Wolf

MEGASIZED BIRDS

The Pleistocene is famous for its megasized mammals. But birds of the Ice Age also grew to enormous sizes. For some island-dwelling birds, a lack of predators allowed them to lose their ability to fly. Without a need for flight, this enabled them to evolve into massive birds. In the late Pleistocene, giant birds were flying (and walking) on Earth.

Dinornis robustus "Giant Moa"

Dates: about 126,000—500 years ago
Range: New Zealand (south island)
Habitat: Grasslands, woodlands, shrublands, coastal areas
Height: 12 feet
Weight: Up to 530 pounds
Diet: Berries, leaves, seeds, shrubs, twigs

The giant moa was a large bird that couldn't fly. It did not even have wings. Size set apart the males and females of this species, with female giant moas standing taller and weighing more. These massive birds hatched from eggs that weighed nearly nine pounds. Humans most likely played a key role in the giant moa's extinction. Just a few hundred years after humans first landed on the islands, giant moas and the other eight moas of New Zealand had all died out.

Merriam's teratorn lived in woodlands, and because of its large size it stalked small animals on the ground.

Teratornis merriami "Merriam's Teratorn"

Dates: 300,000—11,700 years ago
Range: North America
Habitat: Shrublands, woodlands
Wingspan: Up to 13 feet
Weight: 30 pounds
Diet: Birds, lizards, snakes, small mammals

Merriam's teratorn was a predator and could hunt either from the sky or on land. From the air, a soaring Merriam's teratorn could reach 35 miles per hour. But on the ground, its short legs kept it from chasing quickly after prey. Instead, it slowly stalked its next meal. Then, the Merriam's teratorn snatched its prey with its large, hooked beak. It would open its beak wide to swallow the animal, in a single gulp, without chewing. These large birds are related to condors and storks.

EARLY PLEISTOCENE 2.58 million—781,000 years ago						LATE PLEISTOCENE 126,000—11,700 years ago	
2.5	2	1.5	1		0.5		present
		millions of years ago			MIDDLE PLEISTOCENE 781,000—126,000 years ago	HOLOCENE 11,700 years ago —present	
					Merriam's Teratorn	Giant Moa	

DISTINCTIVE ANTLERS

Some animals of the Quaternary Ice Age had truly defining features. Long ivory tusks made mammoths easy to identify. Large armored shells protected the backs of glyptodonts. Woolly and narrow-nosed rhinoceroses had unique horns. Saber-toothed and scimitar cats had menacing teeth.

The Irish elk and stag-moose were two other unique animals of the Ice Age. In the late Pleistocene, these massive deer boasted hard-to-miss antlers. They may be some of the most impressive antlers ever seen on Earth!

Megaloceros giganteus "Irish Elk"

Dates: 300,000—11,700 years ago
Range: North America
Habitat: Shrublands, woodlands
Wingspan: Up to 13 feet
Weight: 30 pounds
Diet: Birds, lizards, snakes, small mammals

No other deer has ever grown antlers as large as the Irish elk's. An Irish elk's antlers could sprawl up to 12 feet across. The antlers alone could weigh more than 80 pounds! Only males grew antlers. The males would have shed their antlers in the spring, only to regrow them again by the fall. They then used them to fight other Irish elk over mates. The Irish elk is not actually an elk. Rather, it is a giant deer. The animal also did not live solely in Ireland. This name came from the many well-preserved remains of the animal that have been found in Ireland.

Cervalces scotti "Stag-Moose"

Dates: 126,000—11,700 years ago
Range: North America
Habitat: Wetlands, woodlands
Height: 6 feet (at shoulder)
Weight: 1,562 pounds
Diet: Plants, soft vegetation

Stag-moose bore broad, branching antlers that were massive and intricate. Parts of the antlers were flat and scooped upward. Other parts featured narrow points called tines. The antlers grew in irregular patterns. The stag-moose earned its name from its odd appearance. It bore similarities to both moose and elk, yet it was neither. It had a longer face like an elk (stag), but its body was shaped more like that of a moose with longer legs. Its antlers were unlike those of either of its namesakes. This browsing animal would have waded through wetlands or walked along streams searching for food.

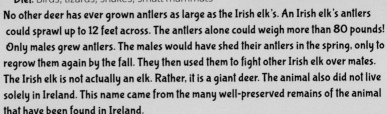

EARLY PLEISTOCENE 2.58 million—781,000 years ago					**LATE PLEISTOCENE** 126,000—11,700 years ago

2.5	2	1.5	1	0.5	present

millions of years ago

MIDDLE PLEISTOCENE 781,000—126,000 years ago

HOLOCENE 11,700 years ago—present

Irish Elk

Stag Moose

LIVING UNDERFOOT

The megafauna may have been the stars of the Ice Age. But those giant beasts shared the Pleistocene with many smaller animals as well. Small animals lived underfoot in every habitat. Many of them still exist or are similar to their relatives that live today.

Dicrostonyx species "Collared Lemming"

Dates: 300,000 years ago—present
Range: North America
Habitat: Tundra
Weight: Up to 4 ounces
Diet: Grass, bark, berries

In the Pleistocene, collared lemmings lived just south of the ice sheets. When the glaciers retreated, collared lemmings moved north with the edge of the ice sheets. Now, they dwell on the Arctic tundra. No other rodents live as far north as the collared lemming. Key traits help them to survive in this cold land. As winter approaches, their summer coat of gray fur changes to white. Fur also grows on the bottoms of their feet and between their toes. Strong, forked claws let collared lemmings dig through snow and ice. In winter, they build tunnels under the deep snow, and their diet changes to twigs and bark.

Lepus americanus "Snowshoe Hare"

Dates: 2.7 million years ago—present
Range: North America
Habitat: Northern forests, grasslands
Weight: Up to 5 pounds
Diet: Leaves, sedges, twigs, needles

Today, snowshoe hares are found in Canada and high in the mountains of the United States. But snowshoe hares in the Pleistocene appeared much farther south than that because of lower temperatures. Large feet let the snowshoe hare easily hop on top of winter snow. It can spread its toes wide so its feet act like a snowshoe. This is how the animal earned its name.

Gulo gulo "Wolverine"

Dates: 781,000 years ago—present
Range: Asia, Europe, North America
Habitat: Tundra, northern forests
Weight: Up to 40 pounds
Diet: Small mammals, carrion (dead animals), berries, roots

Wolverines of the Pleistocene may have been larger than wolverines of today. Wolverines are small, powerful animals related to weasels. Wolverines prefer to live alone. They wander their territories, sometimes for many miles in a single day, looking for food. They either hunt or scavenge depending on what is available. With a strong neck and jaws, wolverines can slice through the frozen flesh of dead animals. Wolverines have two furry coats, the woolly undercoat and the dark, longer outer coat. In the winter, they build dens in the snow to give birth. The young come in late winter or early spring. They stay with their mother for about six months until they are fully grown.

Neotoma species "Pack Rat"

Dates: (Neotama species) 6.6 million years ago—present (Neotama cinera) 1.8 million years ago—present
Range: North America
Habitat: Rocky areas, forests
Weight: 12 ounces
Diet: Mushrooms, berries, seeds, leaves

Pack rats are famous for collecting things. In or near their dens, pack rats build up large piles of garbage, called middens. Their middens hold seeds, fruits, bones, and other things from the surrounding area that the pack rats collect. Middens from Pleistocene pack rats are important to scientists. The pack rat's urine hardened the middens, gluing all the pieces together. This preserved the middens and allowed some to survive today. Scientists take them apart to look at their contents and find out more about the environment the pack rat lived in. Scientists have found middens that were more than 40,000 years old!

	EARLY PLEISTOCENE 2.58 million—781,000 years ago				LATE PLEISTOCENE 126,000—11,700 years ago	
2.5	2	1.5	1	0.5		present
		millions of years ago		MIDDLE PLEISTOCENE 781,000—126,000 years ago	HOLOCENE 11,700 years ago=present	
	Pack Rat	Snowshoe Hare		Wolverine	Collared Lemming	

END OF THE PLEISTOCENE

The final glacial period reached its peak 20,000 to 18,000 years ago. Soon, the planet's temperatures began to gradually warm. The continental ice sheets started to melt and retreat once more. By 11,700 years ago, another thaw spread across the world. A new interglacial period began, bringing with it the end of the Pleistocene and the start of the Holocene Epoch.

CHANGING ENVIRONMENTS

Once more, the environment changed as global temperatures rose. In Europe, grasslands became thick forests of pine, birch, and oak. Forests sprang up in the midwest and on the eastern coast of North America. Areas in the west became more arid. Oaks, almond trees, barley, and other plants that thrived in warm weather spread over southwestern Asia.

A NEW WORLD

As the ice sheets melted, they left behind a new landscape. This happened because glaciers do not remain in one place on land. Instead, they move slowly. As they move, they drag along rocks caught between the gravel and the earth. This debris digs grooves into the land as the glacier pushes forward. When the glacier melts, it can leave behind ridges of the debris it once pushed or carried on its top. These buildups of glacial debris are called moraines.

More extreme landscapes can result from glaciers as well. A glacier's weight and power can carve deep into the earth, reshaping the sides of mountains or creating other new landforms. A retreating Ice Age ice sheet formed North America's Great Lakes. About 4,000 years ago, the lakes had filled with water to reach the approximate size they are today. In Europe, mountain glaciers carved out steep U-shaped valleys. In time, some of these valleys in Scandinavia filled with water, forming fjords.

Fjord

MASS MEGAFAUNA EXTINCTION

The megafauna of the Quaternary Ice Age had survived for hundreds of thousands of years. Some had even lasted for millions. Even so, the end of the Pleistocene brought mass extinctions.

Across most of the globe, dozens of species went extinct over a period of about 2,000 years. About two-thirds of the planet's large animals went extinct. The Americas were struck the hardest. In South America alone, more than 50 types of animals disappeared. North America lost 32.

Australia's mass extinction happened earlier than that of the rest of the world. About 40,000 to 50,000 years ago, most of its largest animals went extinct. This occurred shortly after humans entered the continent.

EXPLANATIONS

1. Three main theories explain why so many megafauna died out. Some scientists point to the rapidly changing climate at the end of the Pleistocene. They think that the large animals were unable to adapt to the new conditions. Changing habitats and a loss of their foods would have put too much stress on the megafauna, leading to their extinction.

2. Other scientists believe humans are to blame. They point out that the extinction occurred shortly after humans moved to those animals' regions. Humans then overhunted their new animal neighbors, leading to the megafauna's extinction.

3. The popular third theory combines the two. Some scientists believe that the stresses from both climate change and human hunters led to the megafauna's extinction. The animals may have been able to survive one stress or the other. Yet both proved to be too much to bear.

However it happened, the extinction of one species likely would have affected the survival of others. For example, the extinction of the mammoths would have affected all animals that preyed upon them. This, in turn, could have led to the extinction of those predators.

Americas

American lion
American mastodon
Columbian mammoth
Dire wolf
Hippidion
Horses (*Equus occidentalis*)
Giant ground sloths
Glyptodont
Macrauchenia
Megatherium
Merriam's teratorn
Saber-toothed cat
Short-faced bear
Toxodon
Yesterday's camel

American mastodon

Glyptodont

Toxodon

Megatherium

Woolly mammoth

Woolly rhinoceros

Eurasia

Cave lion
Megatapirus
Woolly mammoth
Woolly rhinoceros

Africa

Long-horned bison

Australia

Diprotodont
Giant kangaroo
Marsupial lion
Megalania
Palorchestes

Diprotodont

PLEISTOCENE SURVIVORS: HOLOCENE

Today, Ice Age animals still live among us. Although some of the Quaternary Ice Age's most unusual and best-known animals may have died out, many other animals survived the end of the Pleistocene.

Small animals were more likely to survive than the megafauna. They tended to bear more young. This made it easier for them to keep their numbers up, even if many of their species died. Smaller animals also required less food to eat. Skunks, badgers, jackrabbits, and gray foxes are all survivors of the Pleistocene.

Pleistocene survivors are helpful to scientists. When Ice Age remains of these animals are found, scientists can predict certain things about the region in which they were found. Knowing what types of habitats these animals prefer today, scientists can estimate what the climate was like in that region. Knowing the types of foods animals eat today helps scientists guess what types of plants or animals may have lived in the area.

Haliaeetus leucocephalus "Bald Eagle"

Dates: 125,000 years ago—present
Range: North America
Habitat: Near water
Wingspan: Up to 8.5 feet
Weight: Up to 14 pounds
Diet: Fish, rodents, small birds, carrion

Remains of the bald eagle have been found in the La Brea Tar Pits from the late Pleistocene. Fish are the favorite food of these large predators, and bald eagles usually live near water. To hunt, they may perch high in a tree watching the water below. When they see movement, they quickly dive and capture their prey from the water's surface. Hungry bald eagles may also steal meals from ospreys or other birds or feast on the bodies of dead animals. Bald eagles build their nests high in the air—sometimes 180 feet above the ground. Bald eagles reuse their nests from year to year. In time, the nests can grow to massive sizes, possibly reaching 13 feet tall and 10 feet wide.

Mustela erminea "Ermine"

Dates: 300,000 years ago—present
Range: North America, Eurasia
Habitat: Marshes, meadows, woodlands
Length: 13 inches
Weight: Up to 7.3 ounces
Diet: Rabbits, rodents, other small mammals

Ermine are built to live in the snow. In winter, their brown coats change to white. Thick fur lines the bottoms of their feet to keep them warm against the winter's snow. These small, long animals are bold hunters. They zigzag across the ground between cover as they hunt. Often, ermine kill their prey with just one bite to the neck. Ermine will hunt even if they are not hungry. Then, they store their dead prey for later.

EARLY PLEISTOCENE				LATE PLEISTOCENE	
2.58 million—781,000 years ago				126,000—11,700 years ago	
2.5	2	1.5	1	0.5	present
		millions of years ago		MIDDLE PLEISTOCENE 781,000—126,000 years ago	HOLOCENE 11,700 years ago —present

Ermine

Bald Eagle

PLEISTOCENE SURVIVORS: HOLOCENE

Pleistocene's megafauna did not all die out. Some of the Ice Age's giants lived on into the Holocene. Of those, many still live today. These survivors had to adapt to the new world. They had to shift habitats or ranges or find new sources of food. Today, caribou and tundra muskoxen roam the Arctic. The Ice Age's brown bears and elk still spread across the wilds of North America and Eurasia.

HOLOCENE MAMMOTHS

Not all mammoths died out at the end of the Pleistocene. One small population of woolly mammoths survived on Wrangel Island, in Siberia, into the Holocene. During the Ice Age, lower sea levels allowed the animals to reach the island. When the ice sheets melted, the mammoths became trapped on the island. There they survived until about 4,000 years ago.

Ursus Maritimus "Polar Bears"

Dates: 150,000 years ago—present
Range: Arctic: northern North America, northern Eurasia
Habitat: Coastal areas, ice sheets
Length: 8 feet
Weight: Up to 1,600 pounds
Diet: Seals, walruses, beluga whales, birds, fish

Polar bears live much of their lives on the ice. During the late Pleistocene, the animals reached as far south as London. Today's polar bears make their homes on ice sheets in the Arctic. The animal's large paws help it swim long distances, sometimes more than 15 miles.

Polar bears are powerful predators. Excellent hearing and a good sense of smell help them find their prey. Polar bears may wait at the edge of a breathing hole for seals. When a seal comes to the surface, the bear bites into it, hooking the animal with its sharp, curved teeth. Females give birth to twins, and the young stay with their mother for more than two years.

Panthera onca "Jaguar"

Dates: 280,000 years ago–present
Range: North America, South America
Habitat: Forests, grasslands, wetlands
Height: 2.5 feet (modern)
Weight: Up to 220 pounds
Diet: Caimans, peccaries, capybaras, tapirs

Pleistocene jaguars stretched from South America as far north as Washington state. They were one-fifth larger than today's jaguars. After the Pleistocene's end, the animals migrated south. Today, they are only found in Central and South America. Ice Age jaguars likely looked similar to modern jaguars, with golden bodies speckled in black rings and spots. The muscular bodies of jaguars help them to hunt both large and small vertebrates. Jaguars stalk their prey before pouncing. Capybaras, caimans, turtles, and some of their other favorite prey can be found in and around water. Jaguars also enjoy going for a swim in nearby water.

Alces "Moose"

Dates: 150,000 years ago—present
Range: North America, Eurasia
Habitat: Forests near water, tundra
Height: 7 feet (at shoulder)
Weight: 1,400 pounds
Diet: Leaves, shrubs, pinecones, moss

Moose evolved in Eurasia during the middle Pleistocene. They likely migrated to North America across the Bering Land Bridge around 14,000 years ago. Long legs help moose swim, wade, walk through snow, or sprint. Apart from human hunters, only bears and wolves hunt moose. Only male moose have the wide, branching antlers, which they use to battle other males over mates each fall. After mating season, they then shed their antlers. New antlers begin to grow in the spring. These antlers can grow to be six feet across by the next autumn.

EARLY PLEISTOCENE				LATE PLEISTOCENE	
2.58 million—781,000 years ago				126,000—11,700 years ago	
2.5	2	1.5	1	0.5	present
		millions of years ago		MIDDLE PLEISTOCENE	HOLOCENE
				781,000—126,000 years ago	11,700 years ago—present

Jaguar   Polar Bear & Moose

CAVE ART

Since the late 1800s, about 400 sites of prehistoric cave paintings have been found. These paintings were created by humans during the Ice Age. These humans would sometimes paint the walls of caves with depictions of animals they saw in the world around them. In some cases, humans lived in the caves they decorated. Other times, they merely visited the caves. These cave paintings reveal the Ice Age's most famous creatures. Some drawings date back 40,000 years!

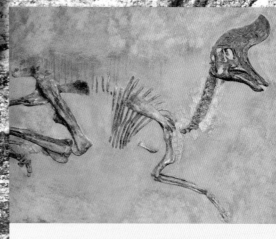

Much of what researchers know about Ice Age animals comes from fossils. Fossils are the remains of animals' bones and skeletons. Researchers use fossils to piece together information about an animal's possible size and habits. Yet there are some things fossils cannot tell researchers. From fossils alone, researchers do not know what an animal's fur or skin looked like.

Scientists use cave art to learn more about the animals. The paintings may reveal which animals lived near the caves, depict how those animals behaved, and give clues about how the animals looked. Some paintings even show if the animals were covered in fur or had patterned coats.

Nobody knows for sure why Ice Age humans made the cave paintings. A popular theory is that humans made them for religious reasons. Other people think humans painted them as part of a hunting ritual. Whatever the reason, cave paintings are a window into the Ice Age.

Altamira, Spain

Discovered: 1879

Age: 22,000—14,000 years old

Animals: Bison, horses, deer, aurochs

The cave paintings at Altamira were the first to be discovered. Drawings and carvings cover the ceiling of the cave. Paintings of horses reach nearly 6 feet in length, while a depiction of an aurochs is more than eight and a half feet long. Along with animals, the heavily decorated walls also bear handprints and human-like figures.

Lascaux Cave, France

Discovered: 1940

Age: 20,000—17,000 years old

Animals: Aurochs, bison, horses, bear, lions, wolves, ibex

Multiple connected chambers make up Lascaux Cave. The massive Hall of Bulls stretches for 65 feet. Depictions of black bears, cattle, and deer are painted on the chamber's naturally white walls. About nine hundred drawings and engravings of animals, humans, and designs are found in the cave.

Chauvet Cave, France

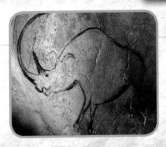

Discovered: 1994

Age: 35,0000—30,000 years old

Animals: Lions, woolly mammoths, woolly rhinoceroses, mammoths, aurochs, Irish elk

Ice Age humans used the cave at two different periods of time, about 5,000 years apart. Two styles of animals also appear, some in red and some in black. Researchers have found remains of Ice Age animals in the cave as well. Skulls of cave bears, wolves, and an ibex were discovered there.

LATE PLEISTOCENE		**HOLOCENE**
126,000–11,700 years ago		11,700 years ago–present

130,000	120,000	110,000	100,000	90,000	80,000	70,000	60,000	50,000	40,000	30,000	20,000	10,000	present

years ago

MIDDLE PLEISTOCENE
781,000–126,000 years ago

Chauvet   Altamira   Lascaux

DEATH TRAP DISCOVERIES

In Los Angeles, California, asphalt bubbles to the earth's surface. It comes from deposits of oil deep underground. These sticky springs create pools on the ground. They are called the La Brea Tar Pits.

The tar pits are a cemetery for thousands of Ice Age animals. They formed a death trap during the Pleistocene. Animals would get caught in the tar pits, and they would be unable to break free from the sticky asphalt. Soon, they would sink into the asphalt and die.

Sometimes predators like saber–toothed cats would see an animal stuck in the asphalt. The cat would attempt to attack and eat the prey. But then the saber–toothed cat would get caught too. Both animals would disappear into the asphalt pool.

Researchers have unearthed more than a million bones from the pits. Remains from about 650 different species of plants and animals have been found. Dire wolves, saber–toothed cats, and coyotes are the three most common animals found. The bones scientists dig up can be more than 40,000 years old!

Wildlife in Los Angeles until 11,000 years ago

La Brea Tar Pits

Discovered: 1901
Location: Los Angeles, California, United States
Age: 10,000–50,000 years old
Animals: Saber-toothed cat, mastodon, Columbian mammoth, Yesterday's camel, giant ground sloth, dire wolf

Researchers first dug into the La Brea Tar Pits in 1901. They discovered the remains of many Pleistocene animals. The asphalt helped to preserve the skeletons. Digging at the tar pits continues. It is one of the best places to find Ice Age fossils in the world.

Victoria Fossil Cave

Discovered: 1969
Location: Naracoorte, Australia
Age: 15,000–500,000 years old
Animals: Marsupial lion, diprotodont, short-faced kangaroo

Ice Age animals tumbled into the cave through a hidden entrance. The entrance was high above the cave's bottom, and those animals were unable to escape. They then died in the chamber. Victoria Fossil Cave holds Australia's biggest, best-preserved collection of Pleistocene fossils. This cavern is part of the Naracoorte cave system. Prehistoric animal remains have been found throughout the system.

EARLY PLEISTOCENE 2.58 million—781,000 years ago				LATE PLEISTOCENE 126,000—11,700 years ago	
2.5	2	1.5	1	0.5	present

millions of years ago

MIDDLE PLEISTOCENE
781,000—126,000 years ago

HOLOCENE
11,700 years ago —present

Victoria Fossil Cave

La Brea Tar Pits

OUT OF THE ICE

Siberia is one of the coldest places on Earth. During the Quaternary Ice Age, animals, such as woolly mammoths, adapted to the Siberian cold and wandered freely there. Sometimes their bodies froze into the permafrost after they died. Now, the world is warming. As the permafrost melts, people discover frozen animal corpses.

Researchers examine the bodies found in the ice. With some, the cold temperatures kept the animal's fur and skin intact. This shows researchers how the animal would have looked when it was alive. Sometimes, researchers can run tests on what is in the animal's stomach. From that, they can learn about what the animal ate before it died. These animals give researchers a clearer picture of life during the Ice Age.

Woolly Mammoths

Multiple frozen woolly mammoths have been uncovered. In 2009, members of Siberia's Yukagir tribe found one. The permafrost preserved its muscles, trunk, and some reddish fur for about 39,000 years. The animal also had an incredibly preserved brain. Scientists were able to compare the brain to that of modern elephants. They found that the prehistoric brain was almost exactly the same as modern brains. This evidence suggests that not only were woolly mammoths highly intelligent like African elephants, but they probably had very similar habits.

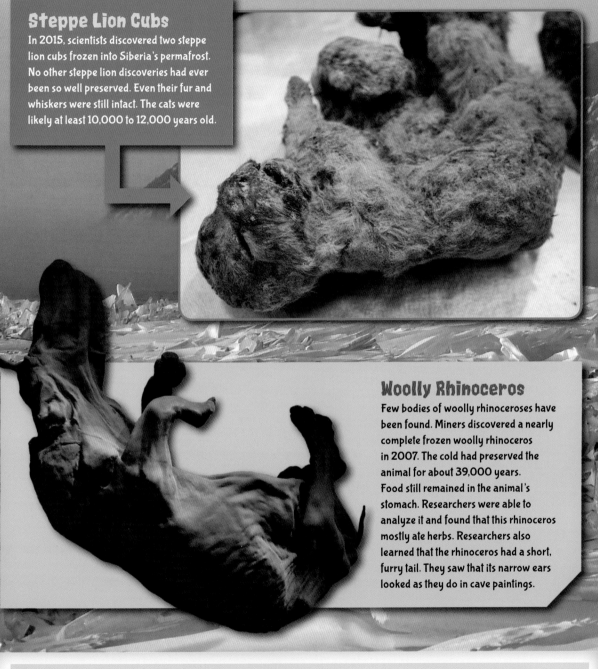

Steppe Lion Cubs

In 2015, scientists discovered two steppe lion cubs frozen into Siberia's permafrost. No other steppe lion discoveries had ever been so well preserved. Even their fur and whiskers were still intact. The cats were likely at least 10,000 to 12,000 years old.

Woolly Rhinoceros

Few bodies of woolly rhinoceroses have been found. Miners discovered a nearly complete frozen woolly rhinoceros in 2007. The cold had preserved the animal for about 39,000 years. Food still remained in the animal's stomach. Researchers were able to analyze it and found that this rhinoceros mostly ate herbs. Researchers also learned that the rhinoceros had a short, furry tail. They saw that its narrow ears looked as they do in cave paintings.

2000	2001	2002	2003	2004	2005	2006	2007	2008	2009	2010	2011	2012	2013	2014	2015	2016	2017	2018	2019	2020

▲
Woolly Rhinoceros
discovered in 2007

▲
Woolly Mammoth
discovered in 2009

▲
Steppe Lion Cubs
discovered in 2015

TODAY AND THE FUTURE

Today, the globe is warmer than it was during the last glacial period. But large glaciers and ice sheets still exist in Greenland, Antarctica, and other parts of the world. This means that the Ice Age continues. However, climatologists believe it may not continue for much longer. Evidence shows that human actions have caused the planet to warm. This human-caused global warming may delay or even prevent the next glacial period.

WHAT IS HUMAN-CAUSED GLOBAL WARMING?

Natural causes brought about the temperature swings of the Quaternary Ice Age and others long ago. Yet climatologists believe more recent temperature rises did not happen naturally. They have found that the burning of fossil fuels, such as coal and oil, contributes to unnatural warming. Gasoline-powered vehicles and a great deal of electricity creation are two leading users of fossil fuels. As fossil fuels burn, they release greenhouse gases into the atmosphere. Greenhouse gases absorb more of the sun's warmth and energy. This means that an increase in greenhouse gases leads to rises in the planet's temperature.

HUMAN-CAUSED GLOBAL WARMING AND THE FUTURE

By 2012, Earth's temperature had risen 1.4°F since the 1800s. Increases since the 1950s are unmatched in recent history. Since 2000, 15 of the 16 warmest years on record have occurred. Around the world, sea levels have increased by about eight inches.

Climatologists believe it is possible that Earth will warm by up to 10°F in the next hundred years. Sea levels could rise by up to four feet, flooding areas along the ocean coasts. Almost all of the ice in the Arctic may disappear. Overall, human-caused global warming could delay the next glacial period, which was estimated to occur in 50,000 years, by 100,000 years or more.

STUDYING THE ICE AGE

Researchers continue to learn more and more about the Ice Age. Ice cores from the remaining ice sheets help them discover more about the planet's climate during the Pleistocene. New studies bring to light new information about the Ice Age's animals. Even as the Quaternary Ice Age's future is uncertain, clues to its past remain on the planet, waiting to be discovered.

GLOSSARY

adapt: to change to become better suited for something

carnivore: animal that feeds on other animals

epoch: an extended period of time

equator: an imaginary horizontal line across the earth that splits it into northern and southern hemispheres

extinction: to die out

fossil: evidence of life from the geologic past. The remains of long-dead plants and animals

fjord: narrow inlet of the sea between cliffs

glacier: thick, slowly moving layer of ice

habitat: the area where an animal usually lives

herbivore: animal that eats plants

ice age: period where Earth has continental ice sheets at the north and south poles

interglacial period: period of warm weather that melts ice sheets

permafrost: permanently frozen ground

plate tectonics: the moving plates that make up Earth's outer layer

marsupial: mammal with a pouch to carry its young

steppe: dry, grassy area

tundra: frozen, treeless plain

WOOLLY MAMMOTH MODEL INSTRUCTIONS

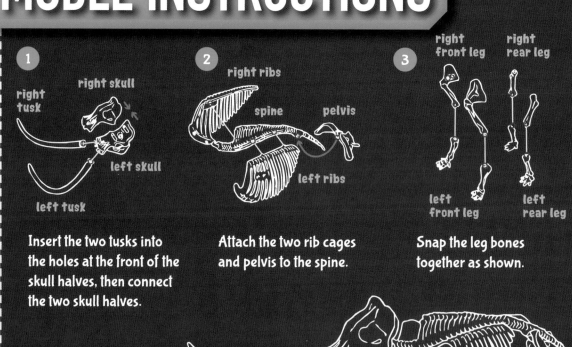

1 Insert the two tusks into the holes at the front of the skull halves, then connect the two skull halves.

right tusk
right skull
left skull
left tusk

2 Attach the two rib cages and pelvis to the spine.

right ribs
spine
pelvis
left ribs

3 Snap the leg bones together as shown.

right front leg
right rear leg
left front leg
left rear leg

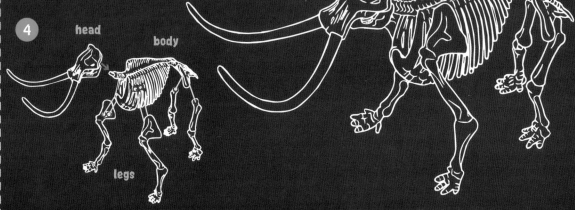

4 Insert the front and back legs into the notches on the ribcage, and insert the back legs into the notches on the pelvis. Then place the skull onto the top of the spine.

head
body
legs

finished model

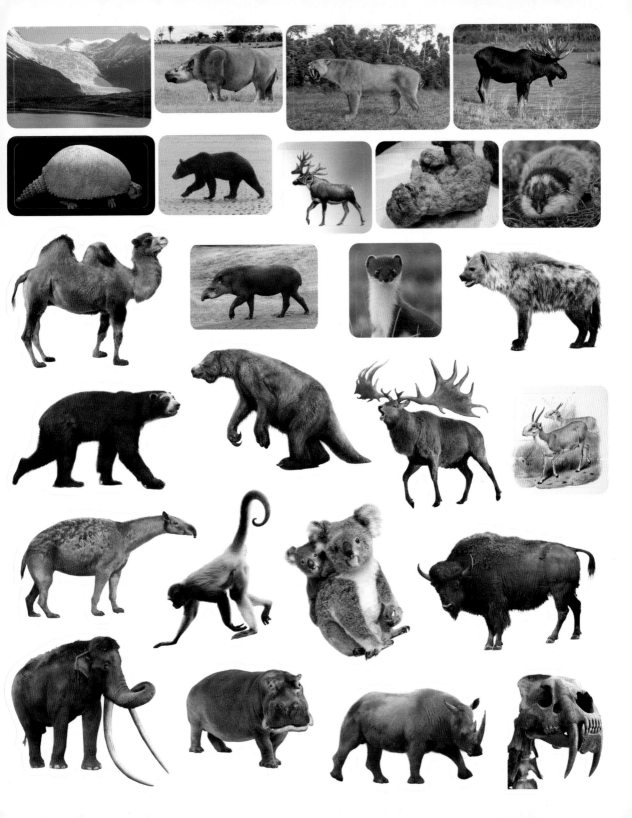